LIFE'S LITTLE
DESTRUCTION BOOK

A Parody

Charles Sherwood Dane

WARNER BOOKS

A *Warner* Book

First published in the United States in 1992 by St. Martin's Press

First published in Great Britain in 1993 by Warner Books

Reprinted 1993

Copyright © 1992 The Stonesong Press, Inc.

The moral right of the author has been asserted.

A CIP catalogue record for this book is available from the British Library

ISBN 0 7515 0098 4

Photoset in North Wales by Derek Doyle & Associates, Mold, Clwyd.
Printed in England by Clays Ltd, St Ives plc

Warner Books
A Division of
Little, Brown and Company (UK) Limited
Brettenham House
Lancaster Place
London WC2E 7EN

INTRODUCTION

Goody two-shoeism hangs like an angel's halo over the land, pressuring us to improve ourselves and constantly do the right thing. Recycling has us going around in circles. Sensitivity shades into silliness. One more rant about co-dependency and we will all go cuckoo. There are just too many good things to do.

Unchecked, the pursuit of perfection threatens to erase the little quirks and foibles and peculiarities that make us *us*. If we become any nicer, better behaved, more socially concerned, blissful – or repressed – we could end up a nation of axe murderers.

Enough already. The prescriptions and advice in

these pages are meant as an antidote to niceness run rampant. The book points the way back towards sanity. Let each sentence be your clarion call. Think small and indulge yourself; vent your spleen lest it explode and splatter your neighbour. Go ahead and be a little obnoxious: make sucking noises; be pushy. Learn again to belittle, belabour and betray. Use more plastic, grind your teeth and experience again the exquisite satisfaction you once knew as a child when you peed in the pool. The future of Western civilization may depend on it.

Along with goodness, there is all too much gratitude in this society, but grudging thanks still must go to the following for their contributions: Victoria Gallucci, Lynne Ward, Gail Girardet, Gene Brown, Sheree Bykofsky, Paul and Chris Fargis, Dawn Sangrey, Bob Detmer and the one and only David Dinin.

1 ♦ Never tip more than ten pence.

2 ♦ Keep the chain letters going.

3 ♦ Post-date all your cheques.

4 ♦ Hum along at the concert.

5 ♦ Take the hotel towel.

6 ♦ Signal left; turn right.

7 ◆ Help fools part with their money.

8 ◆ Don't keep secrets.

9 ◆ Pass on the vicious rumours.

10 ◆ Exaggerate on your CV.

11 ◆ Let everyone know how hard you work.

12 ◆ Practise the art of limp handshakes.

13 ◆ Hire yourself a devious accountant; it's like giving yourself a raise.

14 ◆ Buy this book.

15 ◆ Read other people's mail.

16 ◆ Pay bus fares with £20 notes.

17 ◆ If the mistake is in your favour, don't correct it.

18 ◆ Butter up the boss.

19 ◆ Talk with your hand over your mouth.

20 ◆ Misquote.

21 ◆ Tell the ending of movies.

22 ◆ Use sexist innuendos to get more attention.

23 ◆ Stand up your date.

24 ◆ Give little kids clothes for their birthdays.

25 ◆ Fire people by phone.

26 ◆ Sniff a lot.

27 ◆ Never make your bed.

28 ◆ Cut people off in the middle of their sentences.

29 ◆ Slouch.

30 ◆ Wear jeans to weddings.

31 ◆ Leave the toilet seat up.

32 ◆ Add insult to injury.

33 ◆ Drive at 50 mph in the fast lane.

34 ◆ Park in the disabled space.

35 ◆ Pay by cheque at the cash-only till.

36 ◆ Fumble for change when boarding buses.

37 ◆ Borrow a book and dog-ear the pages.

38 ◆ Put your lights on full beam for oncoming traffic.

39 ◆ Finish other people's crossword puzzles.

40 ◆ Ask people what they paid for their clothes.

41 ◆ Rake the leaves into your neighbour's garden.

42 ◆ Pinch your spouse's love handles.

43 ◆ Don't sign your cheques.

44 ◆ Mumble.

45 ◆ Develop a convenient memory.

46 ◆ Take personal calls during important meetings.

47 ◆ Take your ghetto blaster to the beach.

48 ◆ Remind people that their freckles could be cancerous.

49 ◆ Don't return phone calls.

50 ◆ Use the last square of toilet paper.

51 ◆ Ask people how much they earn.

52 ◆ Don't flush.

53 ◆ Burn rubber at the green light.

54 ◆ Leave a half-sucked cough drop on the new sofa.

55 ◆ Tailgate the elderly.

56 ◆ Tell your kids to try even harder.

57 ◆ Tear articles from magazines in the doctor's waiting room.

58 ◆ Put sticky jam pots back in the cupboard.

59 ◆ Let the phone keep on ringing.

60 ◆ Don't dot your i's or cross your t's.

61 ◆ Carve your name on park benches.

62 ◆ Leave your thumb prints on photographs.

63 ◆ Hold off paying the bills which don't charge interest.

64 ◆ Send anonymous letters.

65 ◆ Drink from other people's glasses.

66 ◆ Develop a truly tasteless foul mouth.

67 ◆ Drum your fingers during other people's presentations.

68 ♦ Leave the concert during the solo or before the applause starts.

69 ♦ Leave the price tags on presents.

70 ♦ Name drop.

71 ♦ Blow out other people's birthday candles.

72 ♦ Don't refill the ice-cube tray.

73 ◆ Leave dairy products open in the refrigerator.

74 ◆ Don't leave a message at the beep.

75 ◆ Talk with your finger in people's faces.

76 ◆ Sleep until noon every day.

77 ◆ Smoke in bed.

78 ◆ Dress 15 years younger.

79 ◆ Forget to wash in the morning.

80 ◆ Be a day late for your anniversary.

81 ◆ Always be right.

82 ◆ Lean on the doorbell.

83 ◆ If there is going to be a fight, make sure you start it.

84 ◆ Don't take "no" for an answer.

85 ◆ Ignore "No Smoking" signs.

86 ◆ Bark orders.

87 ◆ Put coal in Christmas stockings.

88 ◆ Sneer at people who try hard.

89 ◆ Assume everybody agrees with you, but keep trying to convince them.

90 ◆ Brag a lot.

91 ◆ Leave your supermarket trolley on the street or in the car park.

92 ◆ Pledge money that you won't be sending.

93 ◆ Leave desk drawers and filing cabinets open.

94 ◆ Don't vote.

95 ◆ Wash whites with coloureds.

96 ◆ Use gift wrapping paper a second time.

97 ◆ Crack your knuckles.

98 ◆ Follow the letter of the law, not the spirit.

99 ◆ Reserve compliments for people who can do you some good.

100 ◆ Treat underlings as such.

101 ◆ Argue with everybody.

102 ◆ Touch the paintings in the gallery.

103 ◆ Get hysterical.

104 ◆ Block the entrances of lifts, buses and the Underground.

105 ◆ Insinuate, implicate and insist.

106 ◆ Threaten legal action.

107 ◆ Pass the buck.

108 ◆ Eat fruit at the greengrocer; don't buy it.

109 ◆ Flaunt it.

110 ◆ Toss trousers with tissues in the pockets into the washing machine.

111 ◆ Prevaricate, obfuscate and complicate.

112 ◆ Remember that your teen-ager is still a child when buying tickets or paying fares.

113 ♦ Use only American spelling and punctuation.

114 ♦ Gamble with the rent money.

115 ♦ Record over a borrowed videotape.

116 ♦ Tell people they are in your will even if they aren't.

117 ♦ Nurture conspiracy theories.

118 ◆ Don't get caught.

119 ◆ Ask for a rush job except when there is a charge.

120 ◆ Stay directly in front of or behind fire engines and ambulances.

121 ◆ Don't cross until the amber light starts flashing.

122 ◆ When giving directions, leave out a turn or two.

123 ◆ Dream up special requests for waiters and waitresses.

124 ◆ Every umbrella is yours.

125 ◆ Pry.

126 ◆ Don't make up your mind.

127 ◆ Practise passive aggression.

128 ◆ Toss things out of the car window:
tissues, cigarettes, sweet wrappers and
those sorts of little things.

129 ◆ Try whining.

130 ◆ Improve your posture by walking with
your nose in the air.

131 ◆ Remind people who lose their job that they probably should have worked harder.

132 ◆ Accuse, confuse and refuse.

133 ◆ Prophesy woe, financial chaos and domination by Germany.

134 ◆ Leave the Christmas decorations up until March or April.

135 ◆ Talk with your mouth full.

136 ◆ Comment on weight gain in others.

137 ◆ Ask her if the diamond ring is real.

138 ◆ Keep a store of wisecracks for tense and serious occasions.

139 ◆ Pound the table.

140 ◆ Try the expert trail the day you first put on skis.

141 ◆ Scratch your spots whenever you want.

142 ◆ If it feels good, do it.

143 ◆ Answer a question with a question.

144 ◆ See what it takes to get a fellow passenger to pull the communication cord.

145 ◆ Serve corn on the cob to people with dentures.

146 ◆ Don't give to charities unless you get something back.

147 ◆ If you have to give blood, at least make a big show of it.

148 ◆ Have your secretary do all your personal shopping.

149 ◆ Ask the air stewardess a question every five minutes or so.

150 ◆ Assume that your place is
next to the hostess.

151 ◆ Add the straw that breaks the camel's back.

152 ◆ Clean your fingernails at the dinner table.

153 ◆ Take but don't pass on phone messages.

154 ◆ Stopping for red lights after midnight is a waste of precious time.

155 ◆ Tuck a twenty-pound note or two in with your driving licence so the traffic cop will take the hint.

156 ◆ Tell people what you think they want to hear.

157 ◆ Notice good ideas and pass them off as your own.

158 ◆ Smuggle a little.

159 ◆ Put the gals in the office in charge of the coffee.

160 ◆ Make jokes about terrorists at the boarding gate.

161 ◆ See if you can be the first one off the plane even if you are sitting by the window.

162 ◆ Put a title like Lord or Doctor before your name when making dinner and hotel reservations.

163 ◆ Balance your bank account every six months or so.

164 ◆ Have an alias and the IDs to prove it.

165 ◆ Keep two sets of books.

166 ◆ Don't volunteer for the back seat and never take the middle one.

167 ◆ Leave town.

168 ◆ Leave the lights on.

169 ◆ Before leaving the lift, push all the buttons.

170 ◆ Give unsolicited advice.

171 ◆ Don't do anything until you have been asked twice.

172 ◆ Put off until tomorrow whatever you can do the day after tomorrow.

173 ◆ Spot test "Wet Paint" signs.

174 ◆ Say "you know" at the end of sentences, you know?

175 ◆ Don't shower after exercising.

176 ◆ Go up the down escalator.

177 ◆ Develop at least three strategies for cutting into the front of queues.

178 ◆ Change channels without asking.

179 ◆ Underline in other people's books.

180 ◆ Goose the bride and the groom.

181 ◆ Call the wife "the little woman".

182 ◆ Lie about your age.

183 ◆ Tell people what you expect them to give you for your birthday.

184 ◆ If you can't think of something nice, say something nasty.

185 ◆ Slurp your soup.

186 ◆ Be judgmental.

187 ◆ Snap your chewing gum.

188 ◆ Focus on winning and to Hell with how you play the game.

189 ◆ Squeeze the toothpaste from the top and, while you're at it, leave the cap off.

190 ◆ Free cable TV is only a shady electrician away.

191 ◆ Send smutty cards to your in-laws.

192 ◆ Open umbrellas in crowded corridors.

193 ◆ Announce when you're going to the toilet.

194 ◆ Read over people's shoulders on the bus.

195 ◆ Hold out until the other man gives in.

196 ◆ Ignore deadlines.

197 ◆ Revenge is sweet; get some.

198 ◆ Borrow money from your mother-in-law.

199 ◆ When it says "Reserved Parking", that means you.

200 ◆ Pad your expense account.

201 ◆ Take the labels off unopened cans.

202 ◆ Adjust your underwear in public.

203 ◆ Cover up your mistakes and pass on the blame.

204 ◆ Borrow handkerchiefs to blow your nose.

205 ◆ Eat all the chocolates until you find the one you want.

206 ◆ Curse the referee at the under-elevens football match.

207 ◆ When you're done with
your gum, stick it under
the chair.

208 ◆ If you do something nice, make sure everyone knows about it.

209 ◆ Bribe kids; they are easy.

210 ◆ Needle, meddle, coddle, diddle, fiddle.

211 ◆ Gatecrash private meetings with a big smile on your face.

212 ◆ Read the paper during family meals.

213 ◆ Be a perfectionist in absolutely everything.

214 ◆ Put an obscene message on your answerphone.

215 ◆ Be ambiguous; it lets you work both sides of the issue.

216 ◆ Measure people by the money they have and the clothes they wear.

217 ◆ Leave your tights hanging in the bathroom.

218 ◆ Dish out the dirt, but don't take it.

219 ◆ Chew other people's pencils.

220 ◆ Support the death penalty for parking violations.

221 ◆ Get a backseat driver's licence.

222 ◆ Apologize a lot but don't change.

223 ◆ Change the rules to suit your needs.

224 ◆ Lie to your therapist and sit in her chair.

225 ◆ Put your cigarettes out in plant pots.

226 ◆ Make your children stand at attention every morning.

227 ◆ Wear T-shirts with gross messages.

228 ◆ Leave your shopping trolley in the queue at the checkout – then go shopping.

229 ◆ Pull the covers over to your side.

230 ◆ Leave wet towels on the bedspread.

231 ◆ Let doors slam behind you – in people's faces.

232 ◆ Cut your toe-nails in bed.

233 ◆ Repeat yourself.

234 ◆ Repeat yourself.

235 ◆ Quote Adolf Hitler.

236 ◆ Don't know when to stop.

237 ◆ Tell teenagers how things were in your day.

238 ◆ Play office politics.

239 ◆ Vividly describe a hysterectomy when the entrée arrives.

240 ◆ Put things back where they don't belong.

241 ◆ Use the whole can of starter fluid on the barbecue.

242 ◆ Hold the lift until you have finished your conversation.

243 ◆ Scrawl your signature on important documents.

244 ◆ Take your colicky baby to the cinema.

245 ◆ Hand out your business cards at funerals.

246 ◆ Have belching contests in restaurants.

247 ◆ Clean your ear with your little finger.

248 ◆ Let your blind date know she isn't up to what you were told.

249 ◆ Make the same mistake twice.

250 ◆ Pee in the swimming pool.

251 ◆ Drive on the hard shoulder until you pass the tailback; then cut in.

252 ◆ Master and practise your best wolf whistle.

253 ◆ Wear large hats during the movies.

254 ◆ Wear golf shoes on newly
polished wooden floors.

255 ◆ Chew ice cubes.

256 ◆ Leave wire hangers on the wardrobe floor.

257 ◆ Always have an ulterior motive.

258 ◆ Push the panic button every other day.

259 ◆ Take the biggest piece.

260 ♦ Expectorate on the pavement.

261 ♦ Walk your pit bull without a lead.

262 ♦ Forget the pooper scooper.

263 ♦ Get up on the wrong side of the bed.

264 ♦ Forget the punchline, but don't let that stop you from telling jokes.

265 ♦ Grumble constantly.

266 ◆ Race the old woman for the last bus seat.

267 ◆ Take cheap shots.

268 ◆ Comb your hair in the kitchen.

269 ◆ Take forever to find your word in Scrabble ®.

270 ◆ Cause gridlock.

271 ◆ Remember that everything was better years ago.

272 ◆ Bring 8 changes of clothing to the gym.

273 ◆ Have net practice near the greenhouse.

274 ◆ Change your mind.

275 ◆ Glue a chip to your shoulder.

276 ◆ Blame the victim.

277 ◆ Put salt in the sugar containers.

278 ◆ Greet each new day with a growl.

279 ◆ Put your initials in wet concrete.

280 ◆ Crack the spines of good books.

281 ◆ Draw moustaches on posters.

282 ◆ Don't rewind videocassettes before bringing them back.

283 ◆ Dangle participles.

284 ◆ Exercise chutzpah.

285 ◆ Whistle a happy tune – over and over again.

286 ◆ Walk tall, carry a big stick, and use it.

287 ◆ Give out other people's ex-directory phone numbers.

288 ◆ Take money from your child's piggy bank.

289 ◆ Install a siren in your car.

290 ◆ Serve turkey burgers, British sherry and semolina pud for Christmas.

291 ◆ Do unto others as you would never have them do unto you.

292 ◆ Have a penny, take a penny.

293 ◆ Be vague.

294 ◆ Grab someone else's taxi.

295 ◆ Walk very slowly, and make sure nobody can get past you.

296 ◆ Assign names to your body parts, like "winkie".

297 ◆ Put advertisements under people's windscreen wipers.

298 ◆ When others are in a hurry, take your time.

299 ◆ Use a lawn sprinkler during a hosepipe ban.

300 ◆ Chase ambulances.

301 ◆ Overstay your welcome.

302 ◆ Hedge and waffle.

303 ◆ Kick sand at the beach.

304 ◆ Serve fish with the head still on.

305 ◆ Touch strangers.

306 ◆ Guilt trip.

307 ◆ Fog up the bathroom mirror.

308 ◆ Tell how awfully big your haemorrhoids are.

309 ◆ Tell little children the truth about Santa Claus.

310 ◆ Hit below the belt.

311 ◆ Bite your dentist's finger.

312 ◆ He who has the gold rules.

313 ◆ Remember the Sabbath and sleep late.

314 ◆ Worry your mother.

315 ◆ Pick your scabs.

316 ◆ Change horses in midstream.

317 ◆ Let the crumbs fall on the floor, and the chips where they may.

318 ◆ Get up early and take your neighbour's newspaper.

319 ◆ Drive like a cabbie.

320 ◆ Point out mispronunciations.

321 ◆ Sneeze in a crowded lift.

322 ◆ Get into a heated argument about the weather.

323 ◆ Please feed the animals in the zoo.

324 ◆ Spring back; fall ahead.

325 ◆ Open the coffin for one last look.

326 ◆ Leave the alarm on when he doesn't have to get up.

327 ◆ Shake up the fizzy drinks before opening them.

328 ◆ Make animal noises in libraries.

329 ◆ Fart in cramped public spaces.

330 ◆ Never forgive nor forget.

331 ◆ Don't tell the committee that you cancelled the meeting.

332 ◆ Ask people how they are, but don't wait for a response.

333 ◆ Cut somebody today, but only if it's undeserved.

334 ◆ Fish on private property.

335 ◆ Leave lipstick prints on people's cheeks and foreheads.

336 ◆ Assume the authority but not the responsibility.

337 ◆ Get your back up.

338 ◆ Think nothing of it.

339 ◆ Appease belligerents.

340 ◆ Don't stand during hymns and anthems.

341 ◆ Be generous with backhanded compliments.

342 ◆ Try looking down your nose at newcomers.

343 ◆ Find good things to say about Robert Maxwell.

344 ◆ Don't put stamps on your letters.

345 ◆ Swear 'til you're blue in the face.

346 ◆ Wait five weeks to deposit cheques.

347 ◆ Borrow your flatmate's diaphragm.

348 ◆ Live in a glass house and throw stones.

349 ◆ Procrastinate and someone else will surely do it.

350 ◆ Eat like a horse and make a pig of yourself.

351 ◆ Drown your sorrows by bending the elbow.

352 ◆ If you can do the time, do the crime.

353 ◆ Believe that numbers and stars influence the way your life works.

354 ◆ Use more plastic.

355 ◆ Put all your eggs in one basket.

356 ◆ Play with fire.

357 ◆ Split hairs.

358 ◆ Let slip the dogs of war.

359 ◆ Cut corners.

360 ◆ Drown yourself in perfume.

361 ◆ Never eat crow, hats or humble pie.

362 ◆ Fish for compliments.

363 ◆ Crack the whip.

364 ◆ Have bones to pick.

365 ◆ Dance fast to slow music and vice versa.

366 ◆ Cook everything with chili peppers.

367 ◆ Drink orange juice right out of the carton.

368 ◆ Burn your bridges and candles at both ends.

369 ◆ Call your spouse by the name of an old flame.

370 ◆ Heads you win, tails you win.

371 ◆ Take bulbs from the landing lights when you need them in your flat.

372 ◆ Pass on the left in traffic.

373 ◆ Put pennies in the collection plate.

374 ◆ Lean way back in delicate old chairs.

375 ◆ Make fun of all accents.

376 ◆ Don't sign your greeting cards.

377 ◆ Leave papers in the copier.

378 ◆ Rubberneck.

379 ◆ Neck and pet in public places.

380 ◆ Ask your parents and grandparents how much they plan to leave you.

381 ◆ Brush the dandruff off other people's shoulders.

382 ◆ Lick the knife before putting it back in the strawberry jam.

383 ◆ Suspect a plot.

384 ◆ Tell long, boring stories.

385 ◆ Be "in conference" all the time.

386 ◆ Pinch kids' cheeks.

387 ◆ Bitch, bitch, bitch.

388 ◆ Get into every photograph you can.

389 ◆ Have a "Clergy on Call" sign made for your windscreen.

390 ◆ Slap people on the back.

391 ◆ Swear this time you mean it – really.

392 ◆ Whisper behind their backs.

393 ◆ Misfile everything, especially contracts.

394 ◆ Remind friends of stupid things they did ten years ago.

395 ◆ Bum cigarettes.

396 ◆ Park in front of driveways and emergency exits.

397 ◆ Don't tear the edges off computer paper.

398 ◆ Let your nose hair grow out.

399 ◆ Don't wash the milk bottles.

400 ◆ Shave every third or fourth day.

401 ◆ Eat crackers in bed, and then move to your side.

402 ◆ Cover your living-room furniture in plastic.

403 ◆ Mix up books on library shelves.

404 ◆ Overtake funeral processions.

405 ◆ Flash your Rolex, even if it's phony.

406 ◆ Tape-record phone conversations and use them later for revenge.

407 ◆ Feed the dog under the table.

408 ◆ Refuse to use the drink mat.

409 ◆ Don't mow the lawn more than once or twice a summer.

410 ◆ Buy it, wear it, return it.

411 ◆ Be unprepared for public appearances.

412 ◆ Ask if a present is returnable.

413 ◆ Overconsume and buy on impulse.

414 ◆ Tell people they have bad breath.

415 ◆ Keep your car moving fast near the pavement puddles.

416 ◆ Call friends during the Cup Final to talk out your problems.

417 ◆ Copy copyrighted software.

418 ◆ Drink hot coffee while driving.

419 ◆ Don't tell vegetarians about the meat in the casserole.

420 ◆ Occupy a café table for hours with one cup of coffee.

421 ◆ Smell smoke often and announce it.

422 ◆ Keep saying, "That's nice."

423 ◆ Wear sheep's clothing.

424 ◆ Open old wounds whenever possible.

425 ◆ Brag about your new fur in a pet shop.

426 ◆ Tell jokes at funerals.

427 ◆ Throw a loud party in the middle of the week.

428 ◆ Convince other people to take risks you wouldn't touch.

429 ◆ Eat out with friends and "forget" your wallet.

430 ◆ Be nothing if not critical.

431 ◆ Practise pulling the wool over people's eyes.

432 ♦ Don't call to cancel reservations.

433 ♦ Sulk.

434 ♦ Be known for your sesquipedalianism.

435 ♦ Quote proverbs in Latin.

436 ♦ Go topless or all the way on public beaches.

437 ♦ Put everyone on the speaker phone.

438 ♦ Play with marked cards.

439 ♦ Develop the skill of cutting people down to size.

440 ♦ Refuse to have a nice day.

441 ♦ Say "uh" after every word.

442 ♦ Write Dear John letters.

443 ◆ Step on the back of the shoe of the person in front of you.

444 ◆ Deception is power.

445 ◆ Alternately raise and lower your voice to make people question their hearing.

446 ◆ Keep asking, "Are we there yet?"

447 ◆ Belittle, belabour and betray.

448 ◆ Declare "just cause" at weddings.

449 ◆ Use up all the hot water.

450 ◆ Beg the questions.

451 ◆ Find the loopholes.

452 ◆ Covet thy neighbour or his wife.

453 ◆ Bet a beggar double or nothing.

454 ◆ Don't knock.

455 ◆ Refuse reverse-charge phone calls from your family.

456 ◆ If you don't get your way, take your ball and bat and go home.

457 ◆ Clean up your boss's desk.

458 ◆ Hog the dryer at the laundrette.

459 ◆ Eat off your date's plate.

460 ◆ Drink your flatmate's last beer.

461 ◆ Shave your legs with your husband's razor.

462 ◆ Use fly spray in the car.

463 ◆ Bite off more than you can chew.

464 ◆ Eat garlic just before business meetings and intimate dinners.

465 ◆ Indulge in character assassination.

466 ◆ Jiggle your foot continuously during job interviews.

467 ◆ Wallow in self-pity.

468 ◆ Never dust.

469 ◆ Make scary faces at babies.

470 ◆ Run amok.

471 ◆ Look over the repairman's shoulder and offer advice.

472 ◆ Put your feet on the table.

473 ◆ Play mind games.

474 ◆ Recommend untrustworthy car mechanics.

475 ◆ Buy and read the *Daily Sport*.

476 ◆ Bite the hand that feeds you.

477 ◆ Open money presents at the wedding and announce the amount.

478 ◆ Tell everyone that they should be in therapy.

479 ◆ Flirt with a friend's spouse.

480 ◆ Lie with statistics.

481 ◆ Say the coffee is decaf when it isn't.

482 ◆ Serve wine in beer mugs or liqueur glasses.

483 ◆ Give distances in kilometres.

484 ◆ Tell a friend who has had a disaster to look on the bright side of it.

485 ◆ Make fun of men who cry.

486 ◆ Leave your fly open.

487 ◆ Throw out the baby with the bath water.

488 ◆ Borrow money from friends and then deny you did.

489 ◆ Put steel-tips on your shoes.

490 ◆ Leave used dental floss on the bathroom basin.

491 ◆ Learn to recognize suckers and sitting ducks.

492 ◆ Don't show up after you offer someone a lift.

493 ◆ Bring a bar of soap to the health-club Jacuzzi.

494 ◆ Disturb the peace.

495 ◆ Stand in the home terraces and cheer for the other team.

496 ◆ Pretend you're listening.

497 ◆ Step on your dance partner's foot.

498 ◆ Don't back up your computer data.

499 ◆ Cast the first stone.

500 ◆ Don't call your mother.

501 ◆ Make sure you win when you play games with kids.

502 ◆ Never acknowledge anyone else's contribution to anything.

503 ◆ Serve red wine with fish.

504 ◆ Don't date business letters.

505 ◆ Jump to conclusions.

506 ◆ Be a bad sport.

507 ◆ Shake with your left hand.

508 ◆ RSVP on the last possible day.

509 ◆ Answer the phone with, "What do you want?"

510 ◆ Put the fork on the right and the knife on the left.

511 ◆ Put people on hold with a Barry Manilow tape playing.

512 ◆ Have one for the road.